Corporate Governance:
A Board Director's Pocket Guide

Corporate Governance: A Board Director's Pocket Guide

Leadership, Diligence, and Wisdom

Eric Yocam, MS, MBA
Annie Choi, JD, MIB
Yocam Publishing LLC
Washington

iUniverse, Inc.
New York Lincoln Shanghai

Corporate Governance: A Board Director's Pocket Guide
Leadership, Diligence, and Wisdom

iUniverse books may be ordered through booksellers or by contacting:

iUniverse
2021 Pine Lake Road, Suite 100
Lincoln, NE 68512
www.iuniverse.com
1-800-Authors (1-800-288-4677)

Because of the dynamic nature of the Internet, any Web addresses or links contained in this book may have changed since publication and may no longer be valid.

The views expressed in this work are solely those of the author and do not necessarily reflect the views of the publisher, and the publisher hereby disclaims any responsibility for them.

All references to people, places, publications, web sites, institutions, and databases are strictly provided to the reader for awareness purpose only. The authors and publisher of this publication neither endorse nor promote any of the references found in this publication over any other reference not represented in this publication.

ISBN: 978-0-595-45192-0 (pbk)
ISBN: 978-0-595-69263-7 (cloth)
ISBN: 978-0-595-89500-7 (ebk)

Printed in the United States of America

Contents

Part II Performance

Part III Trends and Globalization

Preface

Over the last few years, failures in Enron, WorldCom, and Tyco boardrooms have focused greater attention on corporate leadership and governance. In addition, the board of director position is becoming more complicated because there are more legal due diligence requirements from the Sarbanes-Oxley Act of 2002, and boards are expected to employ the business judgment rule (a good faith effort to obtain information) to avoid the class-action lawsuits that are becoming common place.

This book is written for the active corporate director, investors, instructors, students, governance practitioners, lawyers, international readers, and anyone interested in corporate governance.

There have been many publications about the topic of governance, but this publication focuses on the essential topics and presents them in a pocket guide form. This book should not be considered an exhaustive tome of in-depth topics; it's an attempt to summarize the key aspects and provide a practical source for a quick review.

The book is organized in a convenient and easy-to-use guide cover a numerous topics in corporate governance. What sets the *Corporate Governance: A Board Director's Pocket Guide 2008* apart from other lengthy manuals is its overriding goal: this text presents the corporate governance principles in a brief, yet complete and easy-to-use manner. The guide is ideal for readers, at every interest level, inspiring to learn more about corporate governance and with limited time to spend condensing the various aspects, insights and perspectives on the topic of corporate governance. The *Corporate Governance: A Board Director's Pocket Guide 2008* incorporates a number of helpful features:

- *Handbook Format* To make information easy to find, the *Pocket Guide* presents major principles in each chapter as statements of key ideas.

- *Easy-to-use* Clear explanations and a convenient resource for use by leader, practitioner, scholar and anyone interested in corporate governance
- *Latest Research* Every effort is taken to ensure that the content within the *Pocket Guide* is supported with the most recent research from a number of reliable public data sources.

The topics in this *Pocket Guide* were chosen because they are considered key topics for a reference guide of this nature. Bullets under each topic present the main points and can serve as a springboard to further research.

Acknowledgement

A set of supportive family members, friends and professional associates made the work on this publication pleasant and productive. The authors wish to thank everyone for their patience and continued encouragement.

Part I
Governance Overview

Introduction

All corporations require a governing board of directors, but how effective they are is tempered by many factors. A few factors are:

- Good leadership.
- Sharing collective wisdom between directors and management to improve managerial judgment.
- A threat of shareholder litigation in state courts should translate into additional motivation for directors to engage in active governance of the corporation.
- A director's accountability and due diligence in decision-making requires the management team to achieve milestones for the goals and plans the board of directors establish.
- The realization that serving on a company's board of directors is not only a tremendous honor but also a tremendous responsibility.

There has been a growing concern about the effectiveness of a company's board of directors because the added time and attention boards take is not necessarily translating into better governance or even governance that adds value to the business. Even under improved processes and structures, a director cannot claim to have the capability to conduct meaningful assessments and testing in many circumstances, especially with the amount of legal compliance and limited time to process all of the information generated from a company.

Corporate Governance in the 19th Century

- Shareholders concern about administrative pay and stock losses lead to corporate governance reform.
- Most of the large publicly traded corporations in U.S. were incorporated under Delaware law, which is known to be friendly for forming corporations.

- Trade off between rights of corporate boards to govern without unanimous consent of shareholders and statutory benefits like appraisal rights enacted through enhancements made in State corporation law.

Corporate Governance in the 20th Century

- Managerial class expanded post World War II and with the emergence of multinational corporations (MNC).
- Agency theory reflects the concern with the agency relationship, in which one party (the principal) delegates work to another (the agent), who performs that work. Agency theory gained significant ground (Eisenhardt, 1989)
- "The Separation of Ownership and Control" (Fama & Jensen, 1983) established agency theory as the foundation for understanding corporate governance where the company representing a series of contracts.
- "Nature of the Company" (Coase, 1937) introduced the notion of transaction costs into the reasoning behind formation of the corporation.
- The Modern Corporation and Private Property" (Macmillan, 1932) set the stage for conception of corporate governance.
- Post Wall Street Crash of 1929 legal scholars suggests changing role of the modern corporation in U.S. society.

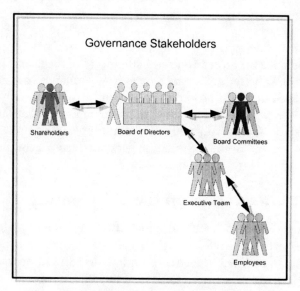

Figure 1—Governance Stakeholders

Perspectives about corporate governance vary, but most of them can be traced to the three theories discussed below. Prospective board members should have a basic understanding these three theories used in the context of the purpose of a board and how well a governance body can govern.

Agency Theory

In agency theory and corporate governance, self-interested directors appropriate value to themselves hence the conflict arises since the director is acting as an agent on behalf of the shareholder. Agency theory is about resolving two problems that can occur in agency relationships.

For example, in the case of a director two agency problems exist:

- the desires or goals of the shareholder and director are in conflict
- the oversight is both difficult and expensive for the shareholder to verify what the director is actually doing on the shareholder's behalf

Chowdhury (2003) suggested when a leader is considering what constitutes shareholder value the leader should also consider that in practice the value proposition might not hold up given the gap present between the stakeholder expectation and the realities of fulfilling that expectation (p. 140).

Stakeholder Theory

Morgan (1994) suggested that with stakeholder theory the existence of complex bargaining process involves multiple interests. The multiple interests (or competing interests) can be found at each level of management within a company including the board of directors. Williamson and Bercovitz (1997) argued that a stakeholder board may be less efficient at generating total benefits. The stakeholder theory defines different groups of interest, sometimes competing interests, yet desire the same end, that is, to receive some type of benefit (Friedman & Miles, 2002).

The traditional perspective on corporate governance (see Figure 1, above) comes from both agency and stakeholder theories (Caldwell & Ranjan, 2005).

Stewardship Theory

In stewardship theory and corporate governance, directors maximize value for the company. The allocation of the board is by shareholders in agency theory, and by the managers in stewardship theory (Turnbull, 1997). Stewardship theory applied to corporate governance means that as an agent on behalf of the stakeholder, a director's motivation is to do a good job with managing corporate assets as a good steward.

Chapter 1

Governance

The topics covered in the governance chapter include, Governance Types, Independence and Committees, Governance Practices, Antitakeover Provisions and Shareholder Rights, Bylaws, Shareholders' Meeting, Block Holders.

In the broadest sense, *governance* is the practice of leadership supporting the decision-making that defines expectations, grants power, or verifies performance. The practice of *corporate governance* is a set of processes, customs, policies, laws and institutions affecting the way a corporate is directed, administered or controlled. Shareholder rights, such as antitakeover provisions, block holders, or anything given in the Bylaws affect how a director can govern, and any director needs to be familiar with these items as they vary from corporation to corporation.

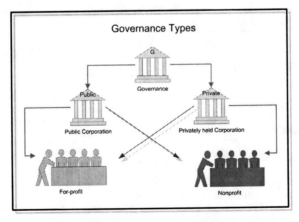

Figure 2—Governance Types

Governance Type

A director should have a solid understanding about how governance applies to for-profit corporations or non-profit corporations (refer to figure 2).

- A *for-profit corporation* is a corporation intended to operate a business that will return a profit to the owners.
  - A *public corporation* is a legal entity permitted to offer its securities (stock, bonds, etc.) for sale to the general public and in most cases through a stock exchange.
  - A *privately-held corporation* is a legal entity owned by one or more company founders and/or possibly their families and/or heirs or by a small group of investors. Sometimes employees also hold shares of private companies. Most small businesses are privately held. In the broadest sense, the term *privately held company* refers to any business not owned by the state.
- A non-profit organization (NPO) is an organization with a specific purpose, such as educational, charitable, or other enumerated purposes. It may be a foundation, a charity or other type of non-profit organization.
  - The United States Internal Revenue Code 501(c) is a special provision where 28 types of non-profit organizations are exempt from paying income tax at the Federal level (IRS, Charities & Nonprofits, 2007). The IRS lists the most common 501(c) organizations, and they include:

501(c)	Description
(1)	A corporation organized under acts of Congress
(2)	Title holding corporation for exempt an organization
(3)	A charitable, non-profit, religious, or educational organization
(4)	A political education organization
(5)	A labor unions or agriculture organization
(6)	A business league or chamber of commerce organization
(7)	A recreational club organization
(8)	A fraternal beneficiary society
(9)	A voluntary employee beneficiary association
(10)	A fraternal lodge society

(14)	A credit union
(19)	A U.S. Veterans' post or auxiliary

Independence and Committees

- Researchers (Klein, 1998; Newman & Mozes, 1999; Shivdasani & Yermack, 1999; Gillan, Hartzell & Starks, 2003) found that having separate committees to nominate, compensate, audit, and govern are more effective ways to monitor governance rather than having the board itself regulate these items.

Governance Practices

- *Governance Metrics International* (GMI) is an organization dedicated to monitoring and rating corporations worldwide on several governance points. The goal of this organization is to provide an easy-to-use tool to show investors and other interested parties how effective the governance practices of a particular firm are.
- Researchers found that the United States ranks fourth for governance practices, but Canada, Britain and Australia placed in the top three respectively out of the 45 countries represented in the GMI ranking (Holstein, 2006)
- Morris, Brotherridge & Urbanski (2005) found that boards that fell short of shareholder expectation include General Motors, IBM, Westinghouse, Kmart, Digital Equipment Corporation, Bre X, Credit Suisse, First Boston, Credit Lyonnais, Adelphia, Paramalat, Enron, WorldCom and Tyco.
- The same researchers (Morris et al., 2005) found that a set of boards that have met shareholder expectation include Citicorp, General Electric, Warner-Lambert, TRW, KeraVision, and the Royal Bank of Canada.

Antitakeover Provisions and Shareholder Rights

- Gompers, Ishii & Metrick (2003) found that weak shareholder rights and the existence of *antitakeover provisions* indicate weak governance. Strong and effective corporate governance is the ideal state for the board.

Bylaws

*   The *bylaws* contain detailed management provisions and rules for directors, officers, and shareholders charged with corporate governance. They provide the structure and rules for governance.
*   The bylaws include time and place of annual shareholder's meeting, time and place of director's meetings, the specific modality and notices for calling special meetings, board of director's structure including the making of committees, the duties of officers and directors, voting and quorum provisions, and many others (Cheeseman, 2003).

Shareholders' Meeting

*   A *shareholders' meeting* is a gathering of all the shareholders of a corporation in order to (1) elect the Board of Directors and (2) hear reports on the company's business performance. It is usually held annually but can be held more often.
*   This meeting is part of good governance because the board is accountable to the shareholders.
*   Creech's (2006) suggests that SEC is looking into strengthening shareholder rights to help preserve the integrity of the director position as well as ensure more effective corporate governance through shareholder accountability and Board transparency.
*   Block holders and other influential shareholder groups can influence decisions at the shareholders' meeting
*   *Block holders* are people who have a controlling interest in a company. They have enough control over a block of voting shares so no one stockholder or a coalition of stockholders can successfully oppose a motion.
    *   Researchers found that block holders might be good monitors or influence the management for their own interest. Some Block Holders might have more incentives to monitor than the others (Bhojraj & Sengupta, 2003; Cremers & Nair, 2003). A board member should be aware of who the block holders are and if their agenda is consistent with effective governance practices.
*   Influential shareholder groups support majority voting/proxy advisory
    *   Among the influential shareholder groups in the US supporting majority voting are the proxy advisory firm Institutional Shareholder Services (ISS), CalPERS and the Council of Institutional Investors.

Chapter 2

Board Characteristics

The topics covered in the Board Characteristics chapter include Board Structure, Board of Directors, Board Size, Interlocked and Interconnected Boards, and Succession Planning.

A director should understand the basic characteristics of the board on which he or she serves. The structure, size, and composition of the board all affect the director's ability to govern.

Board Structure

- Ertugrual & Hedge (2005) found that a strong board structure will curb managerial incentives and allow the board, shareholders, and market to effectively monitor managers.

Board of Directors

- The *Board of Directors* are a group of professionals who bring a breadth of skills, experience, and diversity to a company. Typically, the board will appoint one of its members to be the *chair* of the board of directors.
- When selecting a Board of Directors, the following questions should be addressed:
  - What additional responsibilities will the board members have?
  - Will they assist in promoting the company or identifying potential sources of capital?
  - Will the board members also become shareholders?
  - Are there any potential conflicts of interest with the candidates?

- What expertise should the board members have?
- Will they add diversity of experience and knowledge to the company?
- Will the board be compensated for meetings or paid a director's fee?

Board Size

- The *board size* can affect governance. Smaller boards are more effective since they experience fewer communication and coordination problems (Yermack, 1996, Chapter 3). The researcher found several additional items related to board size:
  1. The median board size from 1988 to 1999 was nine.
  2. The target board size for U.S. publicly-traded company is between 8 and 11 directors.
  3. When the Chief Executive Officer (CEO) is older, the board size increases.
  4. The CEO ownership, CEO as founder, CEO involvement in director selection tend to shrink the board size.
  5. The board size is proportional to the company size (as measured by total assets).
- The same researcher (Yermack, 1996, Chapter 3) found that contrary to popular belief, effective governance and good financial performance is not necessarily linked to the number of external directors.

Interlocked and Interconnected Boards

An interesting situation among board membership is when Boards become interlocked or interconnected (refer to figure 3).

- When two CEOs from different companies sit on each other's boards, then it is said that the two boards are *interlocked*.
  - The fear with interlocked boards is that the CEOs can mutually support each other's agenda, including possibly their compensation package, more favorable consideration, influence the selection of new directors, and inability to facilitate social cohesion among other board members.
- When two or more directors sit on multiple boards, then those boards are said to be *interconnected*.

- Interconnected boards may point to groups of directors having a different focus besides shareholder's interests.
- Fich & White (2004) suggest that a board of directors filled with CEO-sympathetic director appointees are likely to overcompensate and under-monitor the chief executive.
- The same researchers (Fich & White, 2004) suggest that mutually inter-locking directorships that are prevalent among firms are responsible for the production of sympathetic directors

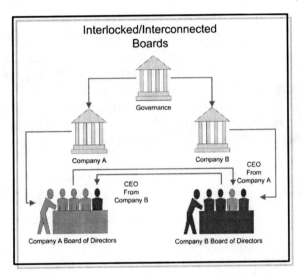

Figure 3—Interlocked/Interconnected Boards

Succession Planning

- *Succession planning* is planning who will fill board positions that become vacant.
    - o   Plan for succession of: the CEO, the senior executive team, and the board itself
- Review board composition and be aware that knowing who will fill key positions should they become vacant keeps the company moving toward its goals.
- More progressive boards are shifting from the short-term, tactical recruit-ing of directors to a longer term strategic approach to building boards in response to the direction and needs of the business.

Chapter 3
Director Characteristics

The topics covered the Director Characteristics chapter include Prior to Joining a Board, Types of Directors, Term of Directors, Recruitment of Directors and Notable Listings, Director Qualifications, Director Expertise, Leadership Skills, Director Trustworthiness, Business Ethics, Ethics Applied: Insider Trading, and Directors and Officers Liability Insurance.

A person awarded the title of director position on a company's Board should feel both a sense of honor and a sense of obligation to the director position.

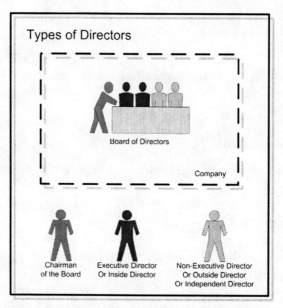

Figure 4—Types of Directors

Directors monitor a company's financial performance and the success of its products, services, and strategy. They are expected to follow developments that affect the business, and set aside any potential conflict between their personal or individual business interests to support the well-being of the business which they serve.

Ideally, directors should have backgrounds and contacts that differ from but complement the background of the officers of the company and of the other directors. The most effective board is a group of professionals who bring a breadth of skills, experience and diversity to a company.

Key components to a successful board are directors with leadership skills, trustworthiness, and good business ethics.

Prior to Joining a Board

- Consider gathering and reviewing the following items before you take on the responsibility of joining a board:
  - A description of the members' responsibilities
  - A brief biography of the CEO
  - A list of the current board members, titles and associated board member affiliations
  - A Board organizational chart
  - The company's or organization's most recent audited financial statement
  - The long-range road map and financial plan
  - A company's annual report
  - A company's or organization's newsletter, brochure, or any available publications
- Evaluate the Directors' Tenure
  - A director's tenure is the amount of time a person holds a governance position at a company and can be viewed as an important indicator of effective corporate governance.
  - Vafeas (2003) suggests that senior directors are more likely to make decisions favoring Management.

Types of Directors

- A *director* is an officer of the company charged with the conduct and management of its affairs. A director may be an inside director (a director who is also an officer) or an outside, or independent, director. Refer to Figure 5.

- An *executive director* is a person dedicated full-time to their role in relation to the management of the company.
- A *non-executive director* is a person considered an "outsider" brought in for his or her expertise, and to lend a more impartial view in relation to strategic decision. They are also called an independent director.
- An *independent director* is a person considered an "outsider to the company". Typically, the independent director position is held by a non-executive director that is a person who is not part of the management of the company.
  - Researchers (Hermalin & Weisbach, 2003; Klein, 1998) suggest that a Board with majority of independent directors is more effective in monitoring the management than a Board with a minority of independent directors.
- *The Chairman* of the Board is a person who leads the board of directors. This person is the presiding director over the other directors on the board. A more recent term for Chairman is Chairperson.
- *The Chairman/CEO duality* is when a single person is both Chairman of the Board and CEO (refer to figure 6).
  - Coles and Jarrell (1997) found that costs of separating these roles between Chairman and CEO by assigning these roles to different people outweigh the benefits.

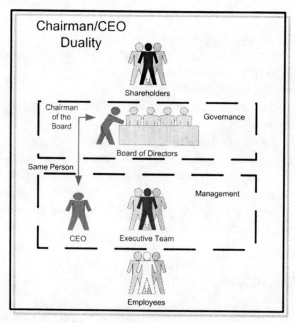

Figure 5—Chairman/CEO Duality

Director's Term

- The *directors' term* is typically for one year, between annual shareholder meetings, unless the articles of incorporation allow for a staggered board (Cheeseman, 2003).

Director Recruitment

- Boards are shifting to more independent management and recruitment is on the rise because the director's requirements are becoming more complex.
- Active CEOs are taking on fewer directorships
- Boards increasingly see recruiting as an opportunity to add someone with a defined set of skills and experience that will improve a board's ability to support the strategy.
    - o   Finding directors with technology or marketing expertise as well as international background is the trend.
    - o   The numbers of women and minority directors still fall short of the levels desired by boards within the United States

Notable Director Listings

- It is hard to find qualified directors given the increased responsibility and SOX compliance.
- A number of director sources are available to find a particular director. The notable Director listing services include
    - ZapData.com—*www.zapdata.com*
    - Hoovers.com—*www.Hoovers.com*

Director Qualifications

- A set of *director qualifications* establish the standard from which a director candidate must be judged in order to hold a governance position.
- Director qualifications vary among companies. However, a general set of qualifications demonstrating, at a minimum, the following
    - Notable or significant achievements in business, education or public service

- Possess the requisite intelligence, education and experience to make a significant contribution to the Board
- Brings a range of skills, diverse perspectives and backgrounds to its deliberations
- Possess the highest ethical standards, a strong sense of professionalism and intense dedication to serving the interests of the stockholders.
- The following attributes or qualifications will be considered by the Governance in evaluating a person's candidacy for membership on the Board:
    1. A past or current leadership role in a major public company or recognized privately held entity
    2. A past or current leadership role at a prominent educational institution or senior faculty position in an area of study important or relevant to the company
    3. A past elected or appointed senior government position or current senior managerial or advisory position with a highly visible non-profit organization.
- Skilled and diverse background must possess the aptitude or experience and should include, at a minimum:
    - To understand fully the legal responsibilities of a director and the governance processes of a public company
    - The personal qualities to be able to make a substantial active contribution to Board deliberations
    - Self-assuredness, interpersonal and communication skills, courage and inquisitiveness.
    - Consideration should be given to financial management, reporting and control expertise or other experience that would qualify the candidate as a "financial expert" under established standards, and international experience.
- Essential characteristics for each board member:
    o The highest standards of moral and ethical character and personal integrity
    o An independence, objectivity and an intense dedication to serve as a representative of the stockholders
    o A personal commitment to the company's principles and values
    o Impeccable corporate governance credentials.

Expertise

- Researchers have found that each director collectively possesses the transformational influence that establishes the values-based climate through which ethical values, expectations with ethical conduct, legal compliance, social-responsibility thereby significantly influencing employees' attitudes and behaviors as well as shareholder perception (Arjoon, 2006).
- *Domain knowledge* is a person's accumulation of expertise in a particular subject areas based on his or her experience, education and skills. A director's domain knowledge requires the director to understand the decision-making from various perspectives in addition to his or her domain knowledge
- Common director knowledge domains include the following:
  - Accounting
  - Advertising
  - Competitor intelligence
  - Core product technology
  - Corporate governance
  - Distribution/logistics
  - Engineering
  - Finance
  - General management
  - Governmental relations
  - International business
  - Human resources
  - Information technology
  - Labor relations
  - Legal compliance
  - Marketing research
  - Product development
  - Production
  - Public relations
  - Research and development
  - Sales
  - Shareholder relations
  - Turnaround

Director's Leadership Skills

- *Leadership* is the ability to influence, motivate, and enable others to contribute toward the effectiveness of the organizations of which they are members. It is not necessary to be in a formal leadership position to exert leadership behavior.
- Shriberg, Shriberg, Lloyd, 2002 suggest that a distinguishing factor between leadership and management is that effective leadership precedes effective management.
- Schwarber (2005) found that a director as leader must:
  - o   Involve the right people in the decision, at the right time, in the right way
  - o   Use a process that keeps people engaged and on track
  - o   Recognize the power of shared decision-making
  - o   Ask a series of key questions to avoid ineffective decision-making
- Hay & Hodgkinson (2006) have found that leadership and management are both stressful during times of economic downturns yet this presents an opportunity for optimizing operations.

Director Trustworthiness and Leadership Confidence

- A director needs to be both *trustworthy* and embody a *leadership confidence* in others with his or her leadership skills. Other important duties required by the governance position include:
  - *Duty of Obedience*—a director must obey the law and regulations giving them the authority to manage a corporation.
  - *Duty of Care*—a director must use prudent judgment and act with ordinary good faith in self judgment.
  - *Duty of Loyalty*—a director must put his or her personal interests after the corporate interest.

Director's Business Ethics

- A director must incorporate business ethics as part of his or her decision-making since business ethics concentrates on moral standard that apply to business policies, institutions and behavior (Velasquez, 1998, p. 132).
  - o   *Ethics* is the study of morality or moral standards (Velasquez, 1998, p. 8).

- ▪ Ethics are a sort of guideline used daily to motivate you to do the right thing (McAdams, Freeman & Pincus, 1995, p. 43).
  - o *Morality* is the study of standards for either an individual or a group (Velasquez, 1998, p. 8).
- *Virtue ethics* is when a person is typically motivated to do the right thing for all stakeholders and takes action. Virtue ethics drives desirable character traits in a person (McAdams, Freeman & Pincus, 1995, p. 43).
  - o Virtue ethics supports the greatest good for the overall collective (Caldwell & Ranjan, 2005).
  - o For example, various ethical challenges present themselves daily surfacing as a conflict between self and others. A director will come across challenges between personal and professional responsibility.
    - A director must acknowledge that virtue ethics supports corporate governance with an eye on creating the greatest good for the stakeholder collective.
    - Researchers have found that virtue ethics drives desirable character traits in a person (McAdams, Freeman & Pincus, 1995, p. 43).
    - Interestingly, Aristotle argued that virtue ethics is the enabling of a person to live according to reason (Velasquez, 1998, p. 132).
- *Situational ethics* take into account *both* action and context (or situation for the action), whereas virtue ethics focus solely on the action regardless of context

Ethics Applied: Insider Trading

- *Insider trading* is the trading of securities by corporate insiders such as a director, corporate officer, key employee, or holder of more than 10% of the company's shares (Harris, 2003).
- Restrictions for insider trading occur during the *blackout period*, which is any period where the beneficiary of the defined contribution plans are temporarily suspended to purchase, to sell, to acquire, or to transfer securities.
  - The beneficiary is a director or executive officer from trading copy stock that the individual acquired during his or her service as a member of the Board of Directors or employment as an executive officer during any blackout period.

Directors' and Officers' Liability Insurance

* Both directors' and officers' potentially incur risk not only with taking a position on a company's Board but also with the accountability associated with the outcome of his or her governance decision-making.
    * Directors' and officers' liability insurance (D&O) offers individual directors and officers the protection they need from personal liability and financial loss arising out of wrongful acts committed or allegedly committed in their capacity as corporate (parent organization and subsidiaries) officers and/or directors.
    * Most D&O policies also cover the liability of the corporate entity itself if the liability arises out of a claim involving the purchase or sale of the company's securities.

Chapter 4

Director Effectiveness

The topics discussed in this section include Director's Colleges, Director Certification, Director Age, Overcommitted Director, and Celebrity Director Influence.

A director's ability to serve on the board of directors of a company is a tremendous honor and a tremendous responsibility. With this responsibility, the director must seek ways to improve his or her skills as well as keep current on changes requirements of the governance position so attending a directors' college is a very good way to take action.

A director should become aware his or her skills and abilities. The director should seek to build both breadth and depth in governance in order to better his or her governance effectiveness associated with fulfilling the duties of the governance position.

Directors' Colleges

- Directors' College at Stanford Law School—Directed by distinguished faculty members of Stanford University's business and law schools (an ISS-accredited program). *http://www.law.stanford.edu/program/executive/programs/directors_forum/*
- Director's College at the University of Delaware—John L. Weinberg Center for Corporate Governance: *http://www.lerner.udel.edu/ccg/*
- Harvard Business School (HBS) comprehensive Corporate Governance Initiative

Director Certification

- By imposing self-regulation, the company's board of directors can ensure that each director's responsibility to uphold the integrity of the director's position in the areas including agency theory, corporate governance, leadership, business ethics, and legal compliance. One way to support a self-regulation effort is through establishing a minimum competence bar with director certification.
- A director should become aware of certificate options available to help with keeping abreast of changes in governance associated with fulfilling the duties of the governance position.

Certificate of Directorship

- Nationally recognized designation for corporate directors by the National Association of Corporate Directors (NACD)
    - o   NACD is a not-for-profit organization serving the corporate governance needs of directors and boards. Additional information can be found at http://www.nacdonline.org.

Director's Age

- A director's age can be viewed as an important indicator of effective corporate governance (Core, Holthausen & Larcker, 1999)

Overcommitted Director

- A director's commitment to his or her position and the amount of time that requires due diligence in preparation for participating in the governance decision-making can be viewed as an important indicator of effective corporate governance.
- A director who has too many other commitments might be less effective than a director who is less distracted with his or her involvement in other activities not associated with the position (Core Holthausen & Larcker (1999); Fitch & Shivadasani, 2004).
- Directors should look at themselves to determine if they are overcommitted and make adjustments in their schedule accordingly.

Director's Celebrity Influence

- A celebrity is a famous person or a person who is widely known in society and business that commands a degree of public and media attention. Some synonyms of celebrity include hero, luminary, notable or personage. Interestingly, fame and celebrity does not mean the same thing.
- The phenomenon of celebrity suggests that celebrity requires not only fame but also fame with an evident monetary value. In the case of a celebrity director and corporate governance practice, the shareholders' wealth potential is at stake (Rein, Kotler, & Stoller).
- A director's celebrity influence can be viewed as a possible indicator of corporate governance performance.
    - o Rindova, Pollock & Hayward (2006) found that emotional responses, mostly positive, that define celebrity translates into an increase the economic opportunities available to a company from the high-level of public attention.

Chapter 5
Committees

The topics covered in the committees chapter include director include Committee Types and Committee Action.

A director should have a working understanding of committees since a board member is very likely to be either assigned to a committee or even head a committee during his or her tenure in a governance position.

Committees are a way to formally draw together people of relevant expertise. They may have the advantage of widening viewpoints and sharing responsibilities (refer to figure 7).

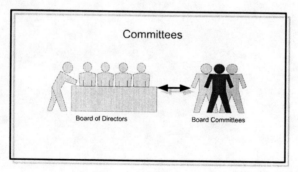

Figure 6—Committees

Committee Types

* The Audit Committee assists the Board in its oversight of the integrity of the financial statements, compliance with legal and regulatory requirements and

ethical standards, and the independence and performance of the internal and independent auditors.

- The Compensation Committee provides oversight and determination of executive compensation, reviews and makes recommendations to the Board about major compensation plans, policies and programs of the company.
- An Executive Committee performs the duties and exercises the powers of the Board of Directors between regularly scheduled Board meetings or when it is not practical or feasible for the Board to meet.
- A Nominating Committee, in conjunction with the Executive Committee, addresses issues such as needed expertise, background, leadership skills, willingness to participate actively, and inter-organizational relationships. The Nominating Committee seeks to ensure overall diversity of representatives and balance of interests on the Board.
  - o Chreech (2006) found that the Board is less likely to be independent when the CEO serves on the nomination committee.
- The Finance Committee assists the Board in its oversight of the management of organization's financial assets, reviews and recommends approval of an annual operating budget, regularly reviews financial results, and ensures the maintenance of an appropriate capital structure.
- A Pensions and Benefit Committee assists the Board in fulfilling its oversight responsibilities related to all company-sponsored savings or retirement plans. The Committee reviews the financial administration of all plans, advises on the proper management of plan assets and liabilities, and assists management in monitoring compliance with laws and regulations governing the management of plan assets.
- The Stock Option Committee oversees the Company's compensation policies and programs, including developing compensation policies, providing policy and benefit plan oversight, administering a Company's various stock plans and the issuance of stock options and other stock-related awards not granted pursuant to a plan, and specifically addressing the compensation of the a company's executive officers.
- A Public Policy Committee researches issues of public policy, prepares position papers and makes recommendations for action to the Board.
  - Ad hoc members are added typically with Board approval to achieve needed expertise on particular issues.
- An Investment Committee develops an investment policy and provides oversight on matters relating to investments made by a company.

- The Planning Committee is responsible for annually preparing a multi-year plan of the company's programs and activities, and recommending priority decision packages into the annual budget.
  - The planning committee periodically reviews and reports to the Board about longer-range plans, including determining when a new strategic plan needs development.
- A Human Resources Committee reviews the employee needs for the company, the company's handbook and the salaries, wages and benefits of the respective employees.
- The Contributions Committee reviews and provides advice to the Board on a company's overall contributions objectives, policies and programs.
- An Environmental Committee assesses the effectiveness of environment programs and initiatives that support the company environmental and advise the Board on matters impacting corporate social responsibility and a company's public reputation.
- The Service and Technology Committee oversees a company's significant technology and services initiatives
- An Ethics Committee is responsible for monitoring the ethical practices of a company, serving as advocates for the ethical practices of the membership, and hearing complaints and making appropriate recommendations regarding violations of the company's by-laws and Code of Professional Conduct to the Board.
- The Corporate Governance oversees implementation of the corporate governance guidelines and principles, reviewing on a regular basis the overall corporate governance and recommending improvements when necessary.
- A Corporate Responsibility Committee assists the Board and management in addressing a company's responsibilities as a global corporate citizen including its responsibilities to its various stakeholders, such as shareholders, customers, employees and the communities in which a company operates.

Part II

Performance

Chapter 6
Organizational Models

The topics covered in this chapter include Centralized Organizational Structure, Decentralized Organizational Structure, Federated Organizational Structure, Center of Excellence (COE), and Strategic Business Unit (SBU).

A director's knowledge of organizational structures and systems are key to optimization of resources and maximization of shareholder wealth. A director should become familiar with different organizational models used to structure the company.

Interestingly, companies tend to vacillate between a strong centralization philosophy and a strong decentralization philosophy in roughly three-year cycles (Ellis & Mauldin, 2003).
An organizational structure and associated culture reflects social factors, technology, and talented individuals (Scott, 2003).

Centralized Organizational Structure

* *Centralized organizational structure* reflects greater number of tiers to the organizational structure, narrow span of control, and a top-to-bottom flow of decision-effecting ideas (refer to figure 8).

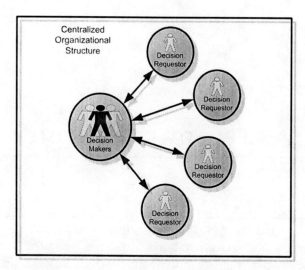

Figure 7—Centralized Organizational Structure

- *Decentralized organizational structure* reflects fewer tiers to the organizational structure, wider span of control, and a bottom-to-top flow of decision-effecting ideas (refer to figure 9).

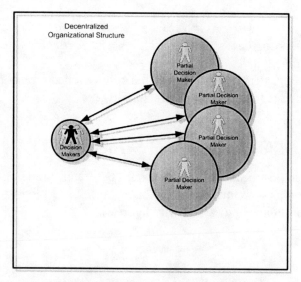

Figure 8—Decentralized Organizational Structure

- *Federated organizational structure* reflects a hybrid structure between centralized and decentralized organizational structures (refer to figure 10).

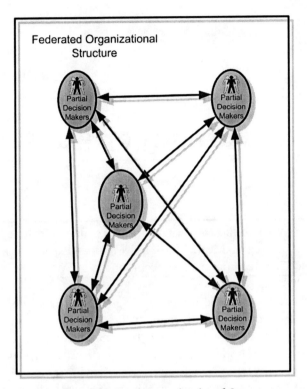

Figure 9—Federated Organizational Structure

- A *center of excellence* is a formally or informally accepted body of knowledge and experience in a subject area.
    o   COE consolidates expertise to maximize talent and productivity.
- A *strategic business unit* can be found within the overall corporate identity. It is typically distinguishable from other business because it serves a defined external market where management can conduct strategic planning in relation to products and markets.
    o   Once a company becomes really large, it is best thought of as being composed of a number of businesses (or SBUs).

Chapter 7

Best Governance Practice

The topics covered in the best governance practice chapter include Governance Principles, Frequency of Meetings, Board Member Participation Checklist, SMART Objectives Technique, KISS Technique, and SWOT Technique.

A director should have a solid understanding of governance best practices in order to ensure his or her effectiveness in the governance position. Over the last few years corporate governance has become an interesting subject, with increasing pressure for both government and self regulation, especially within the high tech industry (refer to figure 11). Laws provide more transparency and shareholder advocacy provides oversight to ensure that the Board is acting correctly on behalf of the shareholder.

First, the United States Congress enacted the *Sarbanes-Oxley Act of 2002* and equipped the Securities and Exchange Commission (SEC) to enforce and address financial stewardship concerns by shareholders with a company's leadership (Creech, 2006).

Second, the *business judgment rule* is a good faith effort to obtain information to avoid class-action law suits by shareholders (Hall, 2004). Interestingly, Business Judgment Rule has important influence with class-action lawsuits and the corporate board of directors.

There is more detailed information about SOX and the business judgment rule in the chapter for Compliance.

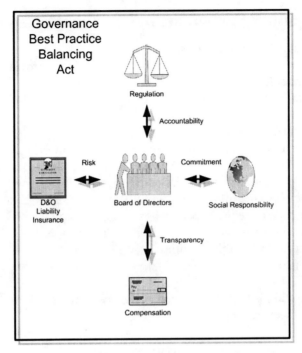

Figure 10—Governance Best Practice Equilibrium

Governance Principles

- A set of principles or guidelines to be used by each person holding a governance position.
    o   Rights and equitable treatment of shareholders
    o   Interest of other stakeholders
    o   Role and responsibilities of the board
    o   Integrity and ethical behavior
    o   Disclosure and transparency

Frequency of Governance Meetings

- Yermack (1996) found that an increase in meeting frequency led to an increase in profitability.

Board Member Participation Checklist

- A check list helps the director stay focus on the task at hand that is to ensure that the director has all the necessary data to make an informed decision. A checklist should include:
  - Attend board meetings
  - Attend committee meetings
  - Read board reports prior to meetings
  - Advice and counsel the CEO outside of board meetings
  - Formally evaluate the CEO's performance on a periodic basis
  - Discuss management succession planning
  - Request specific information not normally included in board reports
  - Determine or request specific board agenda topics
  - Determine or request committee agenda topics
  - Direct internal audit activities
  - Direct corporate compliance activities

Another suggestion is that the director asks discerning questions during board or committee meetings about:

- Financial results and reasons for variances
- Operating results and reasons for variances
- Company strategy or its business model
- Proposed mergers or acquisitions
- Operating budget priorities
- Capital budget priorities
- Internal control strengths and weaknesses
- Regulatory compliance
- Legal issues
- Personnel issues
- Corporate culture and ethical conduct

SMART Objectives Technique

- SMART stands for Specific, Measurable, Achievable, Realistic, and Time-bound. Using this helps the director stay focused on questions during the meetings.
- Specific: Has the objective been clearly defined in terms of what, when, where and how?
- Measurable: Has the measure and use of the measure to quantify the objective been defined?

- Achievable: Can the objective be accomplished or not with the resources available?
- Realistic: Does the current understanding of the objective, resources available and time allotted permit reaching the objective?
  - Time bound: Define the time period for which the objective must be accomplished

KISS Technique

- The KISS method will help the director stay focused on questions during the board meetings.
- KISS stands for "Keep It Simple Sherlock"
- When solving a problem the tendency is to make solution overly complicated
- Use decomposition on a problem to reduce a problem into simpler problems, that is use the "Divide and Conquer" technique to solve a problem

SWOT technique

- The situation decomposition analysis technique uses the Strengths, Weakness, Opportunities, Threats (SWOT) to gain a better understanding of the situation prior to decision-making.
- A director should become aware of situation decomposition analysis in order to understand the importance of critical thinking skills associated with fulfilling the duties of the governance position.
- The SWOT technique helps the director to assess expected internal and external factors such as environmental, political, sociological, psychological, and fiscal changes.
- The internal and external controls ensure that decision-making transparency with the board of directors remains in effect.

Internal Controls

- Monitoring by the board of directors
- Remuneration

External controls

- Debt covenants
- External auditors
- Governance regulators
- Takeovers
- Competition
- Managerial labor market

Chapter 8
Poor Governance Practice

The topics covered in the poor governance practice chapter include Poor Governance, Breach of Duty, and Corporate Crime.

A director should become aware of poor governance practice in order to ensure that he or she avoids pitfalls associated with fulfilling the duties of the governance position.

The inability to self-regulate the code of conduct and business ethics for members of the board requires the government to impose regulations that will not only lead to an impact the make-up and conduct of a company's board of directors but also influence governance standards of companies in countries outside the United States. For example, the Enron Corporation filed the largest dollar bankruptcy petition in the history of the United States on December 2, 2001 (*Business Week*, 2002) and that led to considerable changes in law.

Poor Governance

* *Poor governance* is when the Board of Directors did not live up to the expectation of a company's stakeholders.
* Brook & Rao (1994) found that when it comes to poor governance form poorly performing companies with weak corporate governance in place and those directors are more likely to be sued.
  * Enron Corp.: In 2005, 10 directors paid $13 million
  * WorldCom Inc.: In 2005, 12 directors paid $24.8 million
  * Trans Union Corp.: In 1985, 10 directors paid $1.35 million. The case, known as Van Gorkom, spawned legislation limiting directory liability (Lattman, 2007).

Breach of Duty

- A *Breach of Duty* occurs when the officer of the company, as a reasonable person, failed to execute the duties of his or her position as an agent for the company and on behalf of the shareholders.
- Remedies for Breach of Duty potentially include
    - Injunction or declaration
    - Damages or compensation
    - Restoration of the company's property
    - Rescission of the relevant contract
    - Account of profits
    - Summary Dismissal

Corporate Crime

- *White-collar crime* is when an individual commits a crime while representing the interests of a corporation. These individuals may be employees, executives, or directors. Typical crimes include antitrust violations, all types of fraud, environmental law violations, tax evasion, insider trading, bribery, conterfiting, economic esponiage, money laundering, or trade secret theft.
    - Organized crime—A criminal can set up a corporation either for the purposes of crime or as vehicle for laundering the proceeds of crime.
    - State-corporate crime—The opportunity to commit crime emerges from a relationship between a corporation and the state.

Chapter 9

Compliance

The topics covered in the Compliance chapter include Sarbanes-Oxley, HIPPA, SAS 70, Business Judgment Rule, FCPA, and Patriot Act.

A director should become aware of various compliances associated with fulfilling the duties of the governance position.

There is no single approach with effective corporate governance that produces better-managed companies and satisfies stakeholders' objectives. However, common governance best practices and standards that establish overall responsibility for ethical and legal compliance that align with long-term interests must start with the board of directors regardless of the country in which the company resides (Arjoon, 2006).

High profile failures over the last few years have meant that there is greater attention paid to the corporate leadership and governance, and these failures led to the Sarbanes-Oxley Act of 2002 (SOX). Other regulatory acts are the Health Insurance Portability and Accountability Act, Statement on Auditing Standard 70, Business Judgment Rule, Foreign Corrupt Practices Act of 1977, and Patriot Act.

Sarbanes-Oxley Act of 2002 (SOX or Sarbox)

- SOX is enforced by the Securities and Exchange Commission (SEC).
- The act addresses the shareholder's financial stewardship concerns by demanding transparency with the decision-making from a company's leadership (Creech, 2006).

- SOX contains a wide range of financial reporting standards for all U.S. public company boards, management, and public accounting companies (Arjoon, 2006).
  - SOX contains 11 sections including
    1. Public Company Accounting Oversight Board
    2. Auditor Independence
    3. Corporate Responsibility
    4. Enhanced Financial Disclosure
    5. Analysts Conflicts of Interest
    6. Commission Resources and Authority
    7. Studies and Reports
    8. Corporate and Criminal Fraud Accountability
    9. White collar Crime Penalty Enhancements
    10. Corporate Tax Returns
    11. Corporate Fraud and Accountability
- It requires the SEC to implement rulings on requirements to comply with the new law.
- If a director unintentionally fails to comply with SOX, they face fines of up to $1 million and up to 10 years in prison. Intentional infractions create up to $5 million in fines and 20 years in prison.
- SOX provides *whistleblower* protection
- There are two examples of international SOX equivalents:
  - o In Canada the regulation instruments are 52-109 and 52-111 and in the United Kingdom (UK) the regulation in place is the UK's Turnbull Guidance and Combined Code.
  - o However, other countries have not come as far and both Canada and the UK thereby leaving those other countries with corporate governance structures vulnerable to financial reporting inequalities not to mention an uneven competitive playing field.

Health Insurance Portability and Accountability Act (HIPPA) of 1996

- HIPPA established national standards for electronic health care transactions and national identifiers for providers, health plans, and employers. It also addressed the security and privacy of health data.
- HIPAA (Type I) represents health insurance coverage for workers and their families when workers change or when works lose their jobs.

- HIPAA (Type II) represents a set of national standards for electronic health care transactions and national identifiers for providers, health insurance plans, and employers.

Statement on Auditing Standard 70 (SAS 70)

- The SAS70 by the American Institute of Certified Public Accountants (AICPA) defines the professional standards used by a service auditor to assess the internal controls of a service organization, such as an insurance or health care company, and issue a service auditor's report.

Business Judgment Rule (BJR)

- BJR is a good faith effort to obtain information to avoid class-action law suits by shareholders (Hall, 2004).
- A director loses the protection of the BJR if he or she violates fiduciary duties, which is to take great care in considering all relevant material information reasonably available.
- The BJR prevents the court system from engaging in a post hoc substantive review of business decision made by a director (*Harvard Review*, 2006).

Foreign Corrupt Practices Act of 1977 (FCPA)

- FCPA is a U.S. federal law requiring all companies that are publicly traded stock to maintain records that accurately and fairly represent the company's transactions.
- FCPA requires any publicly traded company to have an adequate system of internal accounting controls.
- The act does not only apply to public companies but also applies to all companies in the U.S. and all of those associated with it.

United States Patriot Act of 2001

- The Uniting and Strengthening America by Providing Appropriate Tools Required to Intercept and Obstruct Terrorism Act of 2001, known as the USA PATRIOT Act or simply the Patriot Act, is an American law that support the fight against terrorism.

Chapter 10

Governance Measures

The topics covered in the Governance Measures chapter include Shareholder Payout, Director's Payout, Governance Metrics, G-score, G-index, ISS, and Other Governance Metrics

Measuring the effectiveness of governance is a challenging task. This chapter addresses how governance can be measured. Even though individually each director has a unique contribution to give to the governance body, the board of directors acting as a whole might not effectively govern.

How does the director know if he or she is part of an effective governing body? One place to look is to how external organizations are measuring effective governance.

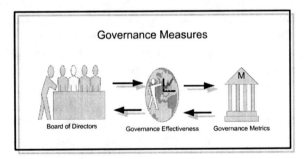

Figure 11—Governance Measures

Shareholder Payout

- Shareholders are concerned with their payout, and a director must ensure that he or she includes this concern in their decision-making process.
- When a Director is considering what constitutes shareholder value and whether it is achievable in theory, the leader should also consider that in practice it might not hold up given the gap present between the stakeholder expectation and the realities of fulfilling that expectation (Chowdhury, 2003).

Director's Payout

- Bebchuk & Fried (2004) have found that a Director's compensation averaged $152,000 per year in the largest 200 companies and $116,000 per year for the largest 1,000 companies in 2002.
- Bebchuk and Fried (2004) suggest that when shareholders require information about the corporate compensation of the company, they are better able to evaluate the effectiveness of the directors and hold them accountable for the salaries paid.

Governance Metrics

- Governance scores from Institutional Shareholder Services (ISS), Investor Responsibility Research Center (IRRC), and Governance Metrics International (GMI) collect data on for-profit companies so the Board of Directors' effectiveness and performance can be evaluated.
- Researchers have found that causal relationship between stock market performance for a company and governance scores and company financial performance (Ertugrul and Hedge, 2005; Gompers, Ishii & Metrick 2003; Core, Holthausen & Larcker 1999; Core, Guay & Rusticus, 2004).
- Beiner et al. (2006) found evidence that suggests a positive relationship between a company's value and the quality of corporate governance.

Governance Index

- The governance index (or *G-index*) provides insight into gauging governance effectiveness for a company's board of directors.

- *Governance G-index* is 24 governance provisions that have been classified into five categories of management power where a higher G-index indicates lower shareholder rights and weaker governance.

Governance Score (G-Score)

- The governance score (G-Score) 51 factors represent either 1 or 0 depending on whether the company's governance standards are minimally acceptable.
- The sum of the 51 binary variables derive G-Score; The score represents 23 unique industry groups; 9 factors in common between Gov Score and g-index include blank check, bylaws, charter, classified board, cumulative voting, poison pill, special meeting, supermajority, written consent.
- The Investor Responsibility Research Center (IRRC) provides the data on G-index.
  - o Investor Responsibility Research Center (IRRC) *http://www.irrc. org*: IRRC's founding can be traced to a protest of the Vietnam War that triggered a rules change enabling stockholders to vote for the first time on shareholder proposals with social connotations. The appearance of those social proposals provoked a need among institutional investors for unbiased, clear reporting on the underlying issues and led to the establishment of IRRC in 1972.

ISS

- Institutional Shareholder Services (ISS) provides clarity on metrics.
  - o The Web site is *http://www.issproxy.com*
  - o Founded in 1985, Institutional Shareholder Services (ISS) is the world's leading provider of proxy voting and corporate governance solutions to the institutional marketplace.
  - o ISS defined 23 unique industry groups
  - o 9 factors in common between Gov Score and G-index include blank check, bylaws, charter, classified board, cumulative voting, poison pill, special meeting, supermajority, written consent.

Other Governance Metrics

- Governance Metrics International (GMI) (*http://www.gmiratings.com*) was formed in April 2000 by a small group of people who recognized the need for a new, easy-to-use tool to monitor corporate governance.
- Boardroom Metrics (*http://www.boardroommetrics.com*) provides governance tools and management services to help improve the performance of business.

Chapter 11
Risk Management

The topics covered in the Risk Management chapter include Why Risk Needs Consideration, Managing Risk, Risk Management Plan, Business Continuity Plan (BCP), and Disaster Recovery Plan (DRP).

A director should familiarize himself or herself with the company's risk management plan. The director should understand various trade-offs associated with the governance decision-making process as part of fulfilling the duties of the governance position.

Risk management is the human activity which integrates recognition of risk, risk assessment, developing strategies to manage it, and mitigation of risk using managerial resources.

Why risk needs to be considered

* Murphy's Law reflects a popular adage loosely that *whatever can go wrong, will go wrong.*
* Sod's Law states that *anything can go wrong, it will.*
* Finagle's Law states that *anything that can go wrong will go wrong at the worst possible moment.*
* Parkinson's Law (Parkinson, 1957) states *work expands so as to fill the time available for its completion.*

Managing Risk

- Once risks have been identified and assessed, all techniques to manage the risk fall into one or more of these four major categories (refer to figure 13):
- *Risk avoidance* may seem to be the answer to all risks, but avoiding risks also means losing out on the potential gain that accepting (retaining) the risk may have allowed.
- *Risk reduction* involves methods that reduce the severity of the loss, such as surveillance cameras to deter theft.
- *Risk retention* involves accepting the loss when it occurs.
  1. Risk retention is a viable strategy for small risks where the cost of insuring against the risk would be greater over time than the total losses sustained.
  2. All risks that are not avoided or transferred are retained by default.
- *Risk transfer* means causing another party to accept the risk, typically by contract or by hedging.
  - Insurance is one type of risk transfer that uses contracts.

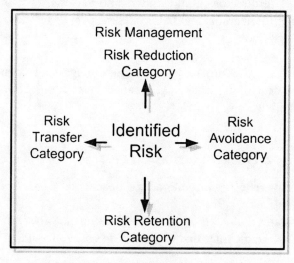

Figure 12—Risk Management Categories

The Risk Management Plan

- The risk management plan should propose applicable and effective security controls for managing the risks.

- A good risk management plan should contain a schedule for control implementation and responsible persons for those actions.

Business Continuity Plan (BCP)

- BPC is a logistical plan developed by the company employees or consultants that details how a company will recover and restore key business processes when an extended disruption in the business process or disaster occurs.
- The plan helps to reduce the operational risk and assess the amount of time to recover.
- Measurable Business Impact Analysis (BIA) and risk management are key tools that employees or consultants use to build and refine a BCP
- The BCP lifecycle includes: Analysis, Solution Design, Implementation, Testing & Acceptance, and Maintenance

Disaster Recovery Plan (DRP)

- DRP is a plan for dealing with unexpected or sudden loss of critical business operations
- DRP is part of the Business Continuity Planning exercise
- Possible events that constitute a disaster include terrorist attack, power failure, fire, theft, human error, equipment failure, and natural disasters.

Chapter 12

Commitment to Quality

The topics covered in the Commitment to Quality chapter include BPI Technique, Six Sigma Technique, TQM Technique, 5 Whys Technique, Cause and Effect Technique, and Taguchi Technique.

A director should become aware of key continuous quality improvement programs as part of building core competencies at a company to help to ensure competitive advantage. A director should sponsor at least one quality improvement program as part of his or her commitment to quality in addition to the responsibility as part of the duties of a governance position.

Building core competencies allow a company to have a competitive advantage because the core competencies allow the company to offer its customers better value than competitors (Afuah & Tucci, 2003).

Constraints and trade-offs (refer to figure 14) associated with the decision-making process reflect a reality requiring leadership at all levels of the company and especially at the governance level.

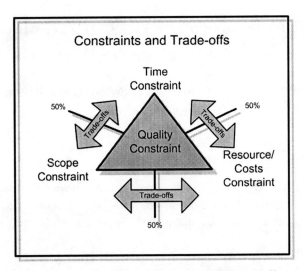

Figure 13—Project Constraints and Trade-Offs

Business Process Improvement (BPI) Technique

- Business Process Improvement (BPI) is a systematic technique developed by employees or a consultant to help any organization make significant changes in the way it does business.
- The organization may be a for-profit business, a non-profit organization, a government agency, or any other ongoing concern.

Six Sigma Technique

- *Six Sigma* is a system of practices originally developed by Motorola to systematically improve processes by eliminating defects
- Six Sigma supports a number of key concepts.
  - o Critical to Quality: Attributes most important to the customer
  - o Defect: Failing to deliver what the customer wants
  - o Process Capability: What your process can deliver
  - o Variation: What the customer sees and feels
  - o Stable Operations: Ensuring consistent, predictable processes to improve what the customer sees and feels
  - o Design for Six Sigma: Designing to meet customer needs and process capability

Total Quality Management (TQM) Technique

- *TQM* is a management technique aimed at embedding awareness of quality in all organizational processes.
- TQM has been widely applied to the following: manufacturing, education, government, and service industries.

Five Whys Technique

- Originally developed by Sakichi Toyoda, the founder of Toyota, the *Five Whys* is a technique of asking a series of "why" questions to explore the cause and effect relationships underlying a particular problem (Ohno, 1988).
  - o A *Five* Whys example:
    1. Our client is unhappy with our service (the problem)
    2. Why?—We did not deliver our services on time to client (first why)
    3. Why?—The job took much longer than we expected it would (second why)
    4. Why?—We made a quick assessment of both time needed and had incomplete set of requirements necessary to complete the service (third why)
    5. Why?—We were running behind on other client engagements (fourth why)
    6. Why?—We have not had time to review both time estimation and requirements gathering procedures (fifth why and the root cause)

Cause and Effect Technique

- Professor Kaoru Ishikawa created a cause and effect technique using a fishbone diagram or cause and effect diagram that maps the cause and effect relationships (Ishikawa, 1985).
- Causes in a diagram are normally arranged categories:
  - o 6 M's Used for Manufacturing: Machine, Method, Materials, Measurement, Man and Mother Nature (Environment)
  - o 8 P's Used for Service Industry: Price, Promotion, People, Processes, Place/Plant, Policies, Procedures & Product (or Service)

o   4 S's Used for Service Industry: Surroundings, Suppliers, Systems, Skills

Taguchi Technique

- Genichi Taguchi developed the *Taguchi Technique* in order to improve the quality of manufactured goods and, more recently, can be applied to bio-technology, marketing and advertising.
- The Cost of Quality (COQ) part of the technique is costs conformance and the cost of nonconformance to which the cost of innovation can be added.
- The cost of conformance reflects the appraisal and preventive costs while the cost of non-conformance includes the costs of internal and external defects.
  - o Cost of conformance includes
    - Preventive Costs—The costs incurred by the company to prevent non-conformance.
    - Appraisal Cost—The cost incurred while assessing, auditing, inspecting products and procedures to conform products and services to specifications. Appraisal costs helps to detect quality related failures.
  - o Cost of non conformance reflects the cost of non-conformance or the cost of having to rework products as well as the loss of customers that results from selling poor quality products. Non-conformance represents costs due to internal and external failure.

Chapter 13
Capability Maturity Models

The topics covered in the Capability Maturity Models chapter include Learning Organization, Capability Maturity Model Integration (CMMI), Software Engineering Institute (SEI), Total Quality Management (TQM), and Pareto Principle—80/20 Rule.

A director should become aware of various capability maturity models to help gauge the maturity of processes used within his or her company. Sustained competitive advantage can be achieved through consistent, repeatable business processes.

An organizational culture that integrates organizational learning concepts where both action and reflection brings with it a richer set of perspectives drives better decision-making (refer to figure 15) within a company (Senge, 2003; Thomas 2003).

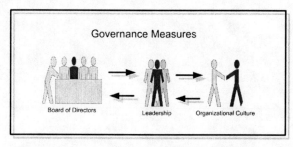

Figure 14—Measurement Drives An Understanding of Capability Maturity

Learning Organization

* A director should consider building a learning organization capability to ensure competitive advantage given globalization and the amount of information available via the Internet.
* Researchers have found that a learning organization supports competitive advantage where the organizational memory requires capturing knowledge from previous situational events with associated decision-making outcomes within the learning organization (Senge, 2006).

Capability Maturity Model Integration (CMMI)

* Capability Maturity Model Integration (CMMI) helps organizations increase the maturity of their processes to improve longer-term business performance. CMMi provides the latest best practices for product and service development, maintenance, and acquisition.

Software Engineering Institute (SEI)

* Since 1984, the Carnegie Mellon Software Engineering Institute (SEI) has served the nation as a federally funded research and development center.

Total Quality Management (TQM)

* Total Quality Management (TQM) is a management strategy aimed at embedding awareness of quality in all organizational processes.

Pareto Principle—80/20 Rule

* The Pareto principle (also known as the 80-20 rule) states that, for many phenomena, 80% of the consequences stem from 20% of the causes (Messer, 2007).
* Example: 80% of a company's revenues come from 20% of a company's customers

Chapter 14

Total Cost of Ownership (TCO) Technique

The topics covered in the Total Cost of Ownership chapter include One Time Costs, Recurring Costs, Project Duration, and the TCO Technique.

A director should understand the mechanics of total cost of ownership technique to help provide insight into a financial benefit/cost analysis. The director should realize that when making any decision that affects the governance of a company that the initial step prior to making the decision requires determining benefit/cost trade-offs.

Total Cost of Ownership (TCO) technique is a financial benefit/cost analysis originated with the Gartner Group in 1987 and has since been developed in a number of different methodologies and software tools (refer to figure 16).

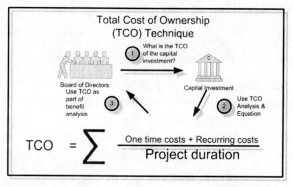

Figure 15—Total Cost of Ownership (TCO) Technique

Total Cost of Ownership Technique

- Total cost of ownership (TCO) is a financial estimate analysis technique designed to help consumers and managers assess direct and indirect costs related to the purchase of any capital investment.
- A TCO assessment ideally offers a final statement reflecting not only the cost of purchase but all aspects in the further use and maintenance of the capital.
- TCO includes the costs associated to the following:
    1. training personnel
    2. failure or outage (planned and unplanned)
    3. diminished performance
    4. security breaches or in loss of reputation and recovery
    5. disaster preparedness and recovery
    6. floor space
    7. power consumption
    8. development expenses
    9. infrastructure
    10. quality assurance
    11. incremental growth
    12. decommissioning
- TCO can also be thought of as the total cost of operation and is a critical part of the cost/benefit analysis process.
- TCO provides a cost basis for determining the economic value of that investment.
- TCO should be reviewed along with other project cost/benefit calculations such as Net Present Value (NPV), Return on Investment (ROI), Internal Rate of Return (IRR), and Economic Value Added (EVA).

One Time Costs

- One-time costs are usually incurred at the beginning of the project in the form of capital expense, or at the end of the project in the form of decommissioning costs to retire capital.

Recurring Costs

- These are costs that are incurred on a periodic basis and originate from the maintenance, refurbishing of capital as well as support of the initial capital investment.

Project Duration

- This is the expected lifespan of the investment. Some companies standardize the project duration one and half to three years, particularly for technology investments because of changes in technology. In contrast, other companies might not include project duration in the calculation resulting in a TCO that reflects a summation of costs that are updated continually over the project's lifetime.

Chapter 15

Board of Directors' Business Intelligence

The topics covered in the Board Reports chapter include Key Performance Indicators (KPI), Balanced Score Card, and Board Communication Tools.

A director should become aware of the usefulness of having access to business intelligence in order to make informed decisions associated with fulfilling the duties of the governance position.

Achieving effective governance practice, the Board members must have timely reports based on an aggregation of credible business intelligence data on the company in order to make sound governance decisions (refer to figure 17).

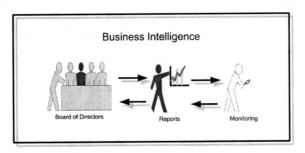

Figure 16—Business Intelligence

Key Performance Indicators (KPI)

* A company must establish its strategic and operational objectives and then choose the KPIs which best reflect those objectives.
* Timing of KPIs, relative to achievement of corporate goals, is fundamental in choosing good KPIs.
* Financial and non-financial metrics used to quantify objectives to reflect strategic performance of an organization. For example, a financial KPI might be to increase average revenue per customer or to increase the gross profit margin. In contrast, a non-financial KPI might be to increase the number customer sales prospects.
* KPIs are frequently used to "value" difficult to measure activities tied to an organization's strategy.
* KPI should measure a continuous or discrete but repeated process.

Balanced Score Card

* Measures a company's activities in terms of its vision and strategies as well as to give the leader a comprehensive view of the performance of his or her business.
* A company's employees provide the input, and the executive team uses it to manage the business and present findings to the board.

Board Communication Tools

* Effective communication is key to any type of relationship. One has to be careful about miscommunications and misunderstandings. Either of these factors is often produce wasted time, hurt feelings, and negative outcomes. So maintaining ongoing communication at work is one element in helping everyone to feel that his or her job is significant and the environment is comfortable.
* Directors Desk is a communication solution for boards. Additional information can be found at the company's Web site, http://www.directorsdesk.com.
* Board Vantage is an online hosted service for confidential collaboration. Board portal supports the management of board communications and facilitates confidential collaboration among members of any group including executive

teams, deal teams, litigation teams, physician teams, and others. The Web site is http://www.boardvantage.com.
- Digital Dashboards, also known as an enterprise dashboard or executive dashboard, is a business management tool used to visually ascertain the status (or "health") of a business enterprise via key business indicators that best represent their business.
    - o   Digital dashboards use visual, at-a-glance displays of data pulled from disparate business systems to provide warnings, action notices, next steps, and summaries of business conditions.
- iDashboards provides enterprise dashboard software. The Web site is http://www.idashboards.com.

Chapter 16

Corporate Governance Institutes & Networks

The topics covered in the Corporate Governance Institutes chapter include Governance Networks.

A director should become aware of various corporate governance institutes and networks to help gauge the effectiveness of the Board as well as his or her responsibility for governance effectiveness associated with fulfilling the duties of the governance position.

Without self-regulation, either the government or an industry will impose regulation. The real opportunity for self-regulation lies in each company's board of directors. They can examine the impact a director's effectiveness in leadership and decision-making skills in the governance and wealth maximization for the company's shareholder.

However, there are a number of corporate governance institutes and networks that can help Boards with determining where to place effort when it comes to effective governances (refer to figure 18).

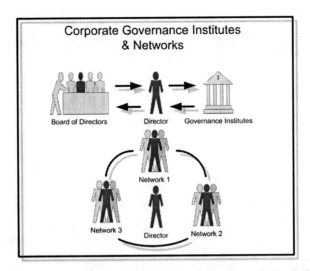

Figure 17—Corporate Governance Institutes and Networks

Governance Networks

- The Board of Directors Network, Inc. (*http://www.boarddirectorsnetwork. org/*) is an organization of women and men representing boards of directors, corporations, government agencies, academia, the legal and financial professions, not-for-profit organizations, and the media seeking to influence public companies to further the advancement of women in the boardroom and executive suites. The Board of Directors Network advocates for more women in both executive leadership and on corporate boards to improve corporate governance through diversity.
  - Institute of Directors (*http://www.iod.com*): IoD is a worldwide association of members and provides a professional business community.
  - Board Source (*http://www.boardsource.org*): increases the effectiveness of nonprofit organizations by strengthening boards of directors through our highly acclaimed consulting practice, publications, tools, and membership program.
  - The Governance Institute (*http://www.governanceinstitute.com*): is driven by its vision for healthcare, its hospital and health system clientele, and its own culture.

Part III
Trends and Globalization

Chapter 17

Governance Trends

The topics covered in the Governance Trends chapter include Globalization, Social Responsibility, Business Process Reengineering, Information Technology as Enabler of Sustained Competitive Advantage, and Ethics Officer.

A director should become aware of current trends in governance. The director should understand governance trends in order to better his or her governance effectiveness associated with fulfilling the duties of the governance position, especially because globalization brings a whole host of changes in responsibilities.

Globalization trends

- *Globalization* is driven from increasing global connectivity, integration and interdependence in economic, social, technological, cultural, political, and ecological spheres.
- *Social responsibility* reflects the ethical rights and duties existing between a company and society.
- The 21st century globalization is placing demands on a company's workforce resulting in a number of trends (refer to figure 19).
   o First, 21st century of globalization places stress on the global business model so the model must address the challenge relating to differences in geography, language and culture (Gupta & Govindarjan, 2004).
   o Second, 21st century of globalization places stress on the company's organizational structure so the company's management must establish a structure that reflects both the decision made by the

company's leadership on the behavior they strive for and how well
the organizational structure works for the company.

o   Third, 21st century of globalization places stress on the company's
workforce so the company's management must make an investment
in Emotional Intelligence (EI) both as part of the HR employee
hiring and retention program through an on-going training program for managers and individual contributors (as part of the proposed action plan in the next section).

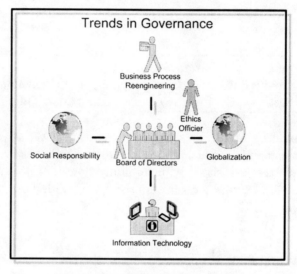

Figure 18—Trends in Governance

The 21st century of globalization places stress on the company's leadership
team to establish a structure that reflects both the decision made by the company's leadership on the behavior they strive for and how well the business
ethics is woven within the organization's cultural fabric in order to work for
the company.

In order to drive sustained excellence a directors should drive the necessity for
building capabilities in terms of multi-cultural leadership and leadership process mechanisms (refer to figure 20).

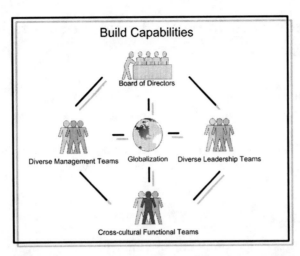

Figure 19—Sustainable Competitive Advantage Through Global Capability

Multi-culture Leadership

- Leveraging a solid multi-cultural and business ethics base, the company's leadership must strive to build global business teams with a mix of members that represent a high-level of diversity.
- Cultivate the necessary leadership process mechanisms that incent all levels of management to strive for sponsoring social responsibility initiatives, like Habitat for Humanity or Green Causes, and aligning a rewards system that benefits individuals for encouraging process re-engineering in order to build global competitive advantage.

Business Process Reengineering

- *Business Process Reengineering* is a management approach to improve processes by looking at effectiveness and efficiency of processes that already exists.

Information Technology as Enabler of Sustained Competitive Advantage

- The evolution in Information Technology (IT), over the past four decades, not only impacted both a company's environment and employees alike but also increased efficiencies from an operational perspective (Mamaghani, 2006).
- Piccoli (2006) found that IT is useful for not only creating a competitive advantage but also sustaining a competitive advantage.

Ethics Officer

- The pressures of globalization have influenced US companies to such an extent that ethics must be considered in decision making. To keep this decision making process in check, the position of *ethics officer* was created.
- In order to address this trend with problematic board of directors', the SEC may let an ethics officer take stronger action on such issues by making a single change in existing law.
  - o   The change could be removing the ethics officer from the management chain of command thereby making the ethics officer directly accountable to the shareholder, just as the Sarbanes-Oxley law has done with internal auditors (Weisman, 2006).

Chapter 18
Global Governance Comparison

The topics covered in the Global Governance Comparison chapter include German Governance, and Family Owned Governance.

A director should become aware of other governance practices outside of those practices used within the United States. A director might find himself or herself on an international Board and might need to understand a different governance perspective associated with fulfilling the duties of the governance position. This chapter does not cover international members of US boards or US members of international boards.

In United States business law, the board is the corporation's ultimate authority. A potential risk is that with most companies, the existing directors, advised by management, control the board nomination process whereby the company's shareholders have little or no input (Time to boot celebrities, enact board reforms, 2005, p. 22).

- Corporate governance various from country to country and does not necessarily follow the corporate governance practices in the United States.
- Japan, China and South Korea have dramatically different corporate governance models than the United States, Britain and Australia (Holstein, 2006, chapter 12).
  - In German corporate governance, a Vorstand is the management board of a corporation where the Aufsichtsrat or Supervisory Board controls the Vorstand.
  - Claessens, Djankov and Lang (2000) suggest that in most East Asian countries, family-owned companies dominate. The top 15 families

controlled over 50% of publicly owned corporations through a system of family cross-holdings, thus dominating the capital markets.

- Likewise, in the Latin model of corporate governance, family-owned companies dominated the list in Italy, Spain, France (to a certain extent), Brazil, Argentina, Mexico and other countries in South America.

Conclusion

The conclusions drawn from the analysis of relevant literature that is publically available presents a broad foundation in support of covering the various aspects of corporate governance. The literature review investigated the historical and recent popular aspects of the characteristics of individual board members identifying any common patterns to suggest that the collective balance of a board member enhances or impairs corporate governance on behalf of the shareholder.

The *Pocket Guide* provides new knowledge in understanding a unique aspect of what it means to be a corporate director. Holding directorship status, from the shareholder perspective, for a member of a company's board of directors is of interest due to potential impact on (1) leadership effectiveness, (2) corporate governance, and (3) wealth maximization of the company's shareholders.

Even though it is not possible to turn back the clock with the event that have occurred over the last few years with failures in Enron, WorldCom, and Tyco boardrooms, shareholders have focused greater attention on corporate leadership and governance. Each year the board of director position becomes more complicated because there are more legal due diligence requirements from the Sarbanes-Oxley Act of 2002, and boards members that do not take action now by taking to time educate themselves with the latest information on corporate governance might find themselves ill prepared for the task at hand especially as class-action lawsuits continue to become common place.

The *Pocket Guide* was not simply written for the active corporate director but it was written for shareholders, investors, instructors, students, governance practitioners, lawyers, international readers, and anyone interested in corporate governance.

Appendix A:
Relevant Books

The board of director position is becoming harder and the director must spend a significant amount of effort to keep abreast of changes in corporate governance.

The list of books representative within the area of corporate governance literature available to the director and provides a sampling in order promote greater awareness.

Title	Author(s)	Publisher	Publication Date	ISBN
Corporate Governance	Robert A G Monks, Nell Minow	Blackwell Publishing	3/1/04	1405116986
On Corporate Governance	Michael Novak	American Enterprise Institute	2/1/97	844770825
Studies in International Corporate Finance and Governance Systems	Donald Chew	Oxford University Press US	1/1/97	195107950
Corporate Governance and Chairmanship	Adrian Cadbury	Oxford University Press	11/1/02	199252009
On Corporate Governance	Michael Novak	American Enterprise Institute	2/1/97	844770825
A Blueprint for Corporate Governance	Fred R Kaen	AMACOM Div American Mgmt Assn	2/1/03	081440586X

Corporate Governance and Risk	John C. Shaw	John Wiley and Sons	8/22/03	471445479
Convergence and Persistence in Corporate Governance	Jeffrey N Gordon, Mark J Roe	Cambridge University Press	4/8/04	521536014
Corporate Governance and Enterprise Reform in China	Stoyan Tenev	World Bank Publications	1/1/02	821351362
Corporate Governance Regimes	Joseph McCahery, Luc Renneboog	Oxford University Press	12/1/02	199247870
Political Determinants of Corporate Governance	Mark J Roe	Oxford University Press	11/1/02	199240744
Dividend Policy and Corporate Governance	Luis Correia Da Silva Domingos, Luc Renneboog, Marc Goergen	Oxford University Press	5/1/04	199259305
Corporate Governance and Capital Flows in a Global Economy	Peter Cornelius, Bruce Mitchel Kogut	Oxford University Press US	7/1/03	195167058
Employees and Corporate Governance	Margaret M Blair, Mark J Roe	Brookings Institution Press	12/9/99	815709447
Cash, Crisis, and Corporate Governance	Victoria Marklew	University of Michigan Press	10/15/95	472105043

The Revolution in Corporate Finance	Hugh Sherman, Rajeswararao Chaganti	Quorum/ Greenwood	8/30/98	1567200877
Corporate Governance 2004	Joel M. Stern, Donald H., Jr. Chew	Blackwell Publishing	5/1/03	1405107812
Corporate Governance in Global Capital Markets	James R Doty	Practising Law Institute	6/26/05	1402404026
Cases in Corporate Governance	Janis Sarra	UBC Press	7/1/04	077481005X

Corporate Governance and Economic Performance	Robert Wearing	Sage Publications Inc	5/24/05	1412908779
Corporate Governance in a Globalising World	Klaus Gugler	Oxford University Press	9/1/01	199245703
It Governance	Lutgart Van Den Berghe	Springer	7/1/02	1402071582
Thin on Top	Jeanne Ross, Peter Weill	Harvard Business School Press	6/1/04	1591392535
Corporate Governance, Market Structure and Innovation	Bob Garratt	Nicholas Brealey Publishing	5/25/03	1857883195
Putting Investors First	Dirk T G Rubbelke	Edward Elgar Publishing	1/1/03	1840648767
Ownership and Control	Scott Newquist, Max Russell	Bloomberg Press	8/1/03	1576601412
Financial Integration, Corporate Governance, and the Performance of Multinational Companies	Margaret M Blair	Brookings Institution Press	6/6/95	815709471
Corporate Governance in Central Eastern Europe	Mitsuhiro Fukao	Brookings Institution Press	4/27/95	815729871
Back to the Drawing Board	Josef C Brada, Inderjit Singh	M.E. Sharpe	6/1/98	765602741
Corporate Governance and Company Performance	Colin B Carter, Jay W Lorsch	Harvard Business School Press	12/1/03	1578517761
Corporate Governance and Firm Performance	Jonathan M Karpoff, Morris G Danielson, M Wayne Marr	Blackwell Publishing	11/15/00	094320528X

Corporate Governance Periodicals

In order to encourage and promote awareness and best practices, the director should invest any available time through self-education and by subscribing to periodicals on corporate governance.

A director should become aware of various corporate governance periodicals to help with keeping abreast of changes in governance associated with fulfilling the duties of the governance position.

Directors & Boards Magazine

http://www.directorsandboards.com/
Thought Leadership in Governance since 1976.

Corporate Board Member Magazine

http://www.boardmember.com
A magazine written specifically for the directors of public companies listed with NASDAQ and the New York and American Stock Exchanges.

Glossary

A

Antitakeover Provision is defensive position taken by a company's incumbent board of directors, which includes poison pill adoptions and antitakeover amendments, found within a company's corporate charter to increase the bargaining power of a company's incumbent board of directors and restrict the acquirer from taking corporate control of the company.

Agency Theory In agency theory and corporate governance, self-interested directors appropriate value to themselves hence the conflict arises since the director is acting as an agent on behalf of the shareholder. Agency theory is about resolving two problems that can occur in agency relationships. For example, in the case of a director two agency problems exist: (1) the desires or goals of the shareholder and director are in conflict, and (2) oversight is both difficult and expensive for the shareholder to verify what the director is actually doing on the shareholder's behalf.

B

Balanced scorecard measures a company's activities in terms of its vision and strategies as well as to give managers a comprehensive view of the performance of his or her business.

Block holder represents a controlling interest in a company, that is to have control of a large enough block of voting stock shares in a company such that no one stock holder or coalition of stock holders can successfully oppose a motion.

Board of directors (BOD) is a group of professionals who bring breadth of skills, experience, and diversity for a company. It also refers to the directors collectively for a company.

Board size represents the number of directors that are participating on a Board of Directors (BOD).

Breach of Duty occurs when the officer of the company, as a reasonable person, failed to execute the duties of his or her position as an agent for the company and on behalf of the shareholders.

Business judgment rule (BJR) is a good faith effort by the director to obtain information to avoid class-action law suits by shareholders.

Business Process Engineering is a technique to improve processes by looking at what already exists and deciding how to improve it.

Business process improvement (BPI) technique is a systematic technique to help any organization make significant changes in the way it does business.

Bylaws contain detailed management provisions and rules binding to directors, officers, and shareholders.

C

Cause and Effect Technique is a quality management technique created by Kaoru Ishikawa. It uses diagrams to map the relationship between cause and effect.

Celebrity is a famous person or a person who is widely known both in society and in the business community that commands a degree of public and media attention. The celebrity possesses one or more traits including credibility, goodwill, rights, image, influence, liabilities, and standard of value.

Celebrity director is an officer with significant influence in the company's governance decision-making and who possesses one or more traits including credibility, goodwill, rights, image, influence, liabilities, and standard of value.

Celebrity goodwill reflects a number of factors including age, health, past earning power, reputation, skill, comparative success and length of time in business.

Celebrity valuation represents the valuation techniques used to calculate the celebrity goodwill including income, market, and asset based.

Center of excellence (COE) is a particular organizational structure that represents either a formally or informally accepted, centralizing a body of knowledge and experience on the subject area.

Chairman of the Board of Directors is a person who leads the board of directors.

Committee is a collection of directors for a specific purpose, such as to manage finances or human resources. There are many different types of committees organized for various purposes.

Corporate governance The set of processes, customs, policies, laws and institutions affecting the way a corporate is directed, administered or controlled.

D

Digital Dashboard is a business management tool used to visually ascertain the status (or "health") of a business enterprise via key business indicators

Director An officer of the company charged with the conduct and management of its affairs. A director may be an *inside director* (a director who is also an officer) or an outside, or independent, director.

Domain knowledge represents a person's accumulation of expertise in a particular subject areas based on his or her experience, education and skills.

Duality with Chairman/CEO position represents the situation when a single person holds two positions at a company both the Chairman of the Board position and the CEO position

Duty of Obedience is when a director must obey the law and regulations giving them the authority to manage a corporation.

Duty of Care is when a director must use prudent judgment and act with ordinary good faith in self judgment.

Duty of Loyalty is when a director must put his or her personal interests after the corporate interest.

E

Enterprise Dashboard see Digital Dashboard

Ethics is the study of morality or moral standards (Velasquez, 1998, p. 8). Ethics are a sort of guideline used daily to motivate you to do the right thing (McAdams, Freeman & Pincus, 1995, p. 43).

Executive Dashboard see Digital Dashboard

Executive director is a person who is a senior manager or executive officer of an organization, company or corporation.

F

Fair Market Value represents the amount paid for a product or service when compared to other comparable products or services by a number of buyers.

Five whys technique is a question asking method used to explore the cause/ effect relationships underlying a particular problem.

For-profit corporation is a corporation that is intended to operate a business which will return a profit to the owners.

G

Governance Index (G-index) is 24 governance provisions that have been classified into five categories of management power where a higher G-index indicates lower shareholder rights and weaker governance.

Globalization is driven from increasing global connectivity, integration and interdependence in economic, social, technological, cultural, political, and ecological spheres.

Governance Score (G-Score) 51 factors represent either 1 or 0 depending on whether the company's governance standards are minimally acceptable.

Governance is the leadership process that supports decision-making that define expectations, grant power, or verify performance.

Governance network is the interaction of individuals who represent boards of directors, corporations, government agencies, academia, the legal and financial professions, and not-for-profit organizations..

Governance Metrics International (GMI) is an organization dedicated to monitoring and rating corporations worldwide on several governance points. The goal of this organization is to provide an easy-to-use tool to show investors and other interested parties how effective the governance practices of a particular firm are.

Governance Type is what type of company you are governing: non-profit or profit.

H

Health Insurance Portability and Accountability Act (HIPPA) established national standards for electronic health care transactions and national identifiers for providers, health plans, and employers. It also addressed the security and privacy of health data.

I

Independent director see Non-executive director.

Interconnected Board is when two or more directors sit on multiple boards, then those boards.

Interlocked Board is when two boards has one CEO that sits on the board of another company and this company's CEO sits on the board of the first CEO's company respectively,

Investment value represents the amount a standard of value for celebrity goodwill.

K

Key Performance Indicators (KPIs) are financial and non-financial metrics used to quantify objectives to reflect strategic performance of an organization.

L

Leadership: is the ability to influence, motivate, and enable others to contribute toward the effectiveness of the organizations of which they are members.

M

Morality is the study of standards for either an individual or a group

N

Non-executive director (or outside director) A person who is a member of the board of directors of a company who does not form part of the executive management team.

Non-profit corporation A entity that is usually created with a specific purpose, such as for educational, charitable or related to other enumerated purposes, it may be a foundation, a charity or other type of non-profit organization.

O

Outside director See Non-executive director.

P

Poor governance is the situation when the Board of Directors did not live up to the expectation of a company's stakeholders.

Poison pill is an anti-takeover provision to force a would-be company acquirer to negotiate with the target takeover company's board of directors. See Anti-takeover Provisions.

Public Corporation is a legal entity permitted to offer securities for sale to the public.

Privately-held Corporation is typically a company that is owned by one or more company founders and/or possibly their families and/or heirs or by a small group of investors.

S

Sarbanes-Oxley (SOX) Act of 2002 enacted by US Congress and enforced by the Securities and Exchange Commission (SEC) to address financial steward-ship concerns by shareholders with a company's leadership.

Shareholders' meeting is a type of meeting held with directors, management, usually annually, with all the shareholders of a corporation to elect the Board of Directors and hear reports on the company's business performance.

Shareholder is a person with an ownership claim of the company where the claim is typically reflected in a company's share of common stock.

Shareholder wealth maximization represents a shareholder's motive in gaining the maximum amount of economic value from appreciation of a company's share of common stock.

Situation decomposition analysis technique uses the Strengths, Weakness, Opportunities, Threats (SWOT) to gain a better understanding of the situation prior to decision-making.

Six Sigma technique employed to systematically improve processes by eliminating defects.

Slate refers to a list of director nominees placed on the company ballot for election.

Social responsibility reflects the ethical rights and duties existing between a company and society.

Stakeholder Theory Morgan (1994) suggested that with stakeholder theory the existence of complex bargaining process involves multiple interests. The multiple interests (or competing interests) can be found at each level of management within a company including the board of directors. Williamson and Bercovitz

(1997) argued that a stakeholder board may be less efficient at generating total benefits. The stakeholder theory defines different groups of interest, sometimes competing interests, yet desire the same end, that is, to receive some type of benefit (Friedman & Miles, 2002).

Strengths, Weakness, Opportunities, Threats (SWOT) see Situation decomposition.

Stewardship Theory In stewardship theory and corporate governance, directors maximize value for the company. The allocation of the board is by shareholders in agency theory, and by the managers in stewardship theory (Turnbull, 1997). Stewardship theory applied to corporate governance means that as an agent on behalf of the stakeholder, a director's motivation is to do a good job with managing corporate assets as a good steward.

Succession Planning means to plan for board vacancies before they occur.

T

Taguchi Technique is a quality management technique developed by Genici Taguci with emphasis on minimizing variation as the main means of improving quality.

Total Cost of Ownership is a financial estimate technique to help consumers and managers assess costs related to any purchases.

Total Quality Management (TQM) is a management technique aimed at embedding awareness of quality in all organizational processes.

V

Virtue ethics is creating the greatest good all the stakeholders.

W

Wealth represents the economic value of an accumulation of intangible or tangible resources.

Wealth maximization represents gaining the maximum amount of economic value.

White-collar crime is the result of a person acting in interest of company but through the person's action commits a crime.

Whistleblower is a person who identifies a law violation, misconduct and/or fraud found and reports it to authorities.

References

Afuah, A., and Tucci, C. L. (2003). *Internet business models and strategies* (2nd ed.). New York: McGraw Hill.

Arjoon, S. (2006). Striking a balance between rules and principles-based approaches for effective governance: A risks-based approach, Journal of Business Ethics, 68(1), 53. Retrieved April 24, 2007 from ProQuest database.

Bebchuk, L. and Fried, J. (2004) *Pay without performance: The unfulfilled promise of executive compensation*. Massachusetts: Harvard University Press.

Beiner, S., Drobetz, W., Schmid, M., & Zimmermann, H. (2006). An integrated framework for corporate governance and firm valuation. *European Financial Management*, 12, 249-283. Retrieved April 9, 2007, from EBSCOhost database.

Bhojraj, S. and Sengupta, P. (2003), Effect of Corporate Governance on Bond Ratings and Yields: The Role of Institutional Investors and Outside Directors, *Journal of Business* 76, 455-475. Retrieved April 13, 2007 from EBSCO database.

Brook, Y. and Rao, R., (1994). Shareholder wealth effects of directors' liability limitation provisions, *Journal of Financial and Quantitative Analysis*, 29(3), 481-497. Retrieved April 24, 2007 from ProQuest database.

Business Week. (2002 May 6). Eroding confidence, Business Week Online. Retrieved on April 24, 2007 from www.businessweek.com

Caldwell, C., & Ranjan, K. (2005). Organizational governance and ethical systems: A covenantal approach to building trust, *Journal of Business Ethics*, 2(58), 249-259. Retrieved on April 24, 2007 from EBSCO online database.

Charities & Non-Profits (2007). Internal Revenue Service. Retrieved May 24, 2007 from http://www.irs.gov/charities/index.html

Cheeseman, H. (2003) *Contemporary Business and E-Commerce Law*, 4th ed. New Jersey: Person Education.

Chowdhury, S. (2003). *Organization 21C: Someday all organizations will lead this way*. Upper Saddle River, New Jersey: Prentice Hall.

Core, J. E., Holthausen and W. R., Larcker, D. F. (1999), Corporate Governance, Chief Executive Officer Compensation, and Company Performance, *Journal of Financial Economics* 51, 371-406.

Creech, D. (2006). Sarbanes-Oxley and Cost Engineering, Cost Engineering. 48(7), 8-12. Retrieved on April 24, 2007 from EBSCO online database.

Ellis, J., Mauldin, T. (2003). Learning in the large enterprise: Centralized vs. decentralized, Chief Learning Officer. Retrieved on April 24, 2007 from http://www.clomedia.com/content/templates/clo_feature.asp?articleid=128&zoneid=30

Ertugrul, M. and Hedge, S. (2005). Financial Management Association. Corporate Governance and Company Performance. Retrieved April 9, 2007 from http://www.fma.org/Chicago/Papers/CGS_performance_fma.pdf

Fich, E., White, L. (2004). Ties that Bind, Stern Business School, New York University. Retrieved November 11, 2007 from http://www.stern.nyu.edu/Sternbusiness/spring_summer_2004/tiesthatbind.html

Friedman, A. and Miles, S. (2002). Developing Stakeholder Theory, *Journal of Management Studies*, 39(1), 1-21. Retrieved April 19, 2007 from ProQuest database.

Gillan, L. S., Hartzell, J.C. and Starks, L.T, 2003, Explaining Corporate Governance: Boards, Bylaws and Charter Provisions, *Working paper.*

Gompers, P., Ishii, J., and Metrick A. (2003), Corporate Governance and Equity Prices, *Quarterly Journal of Economics* 118, 107-155.

Gupta, A. K., and Govindarajan, V. (2004). *Global strategy and organization.* New York: John Wiley & Sons.

Hall, L. (2004). Can fairness opinions protect the board from liability? Corporate Board. 25(144), 22-25. Retrieved on April 24, 2007 from EBSCO online database.

Harris, L. (2003) *Trading & Exchanges*, Oxford Press: Oxford.

Hay, A., Hodgkinson, M. (2006). Rethinking leadership: A way forward for teaching leadership? *Leadership & Organization Development Journal*, 27(2), 144-158. Retrieved April 24, 2007 from Emerald database.

Hermalin, B., Weisbach, M. (2003), Boards of Directors as an Endogeneously Determined Institution: A Survey of Economic Literature, Federal Reserve Bank of New York Economic Policy Review

Holstein, W. (2006). GMI rates governance by country, Directorship, 11. Retrieved April 24, 2007 from ProQuest database.

Ishikawa, K. (1985). *What is Total Quality Control*, Prentice-Hall: New Jersey.

Klein, A. (1998), Company Performance and Board Committee Structure, *Journal of Law and Economics*, 41, 275-303.

Lattman, P. (2007 April 23). Settlement in Just for Feet Case May Fan Board Fears, *The Wall Street Journal*, (94), B6.

Mamaghani, F. (2006). Impact of information technology on the workforce of the future: An analysis. *International Journal of Management*, 23(4), 845-850. Retrieved April 24, 2007 from EBSCO Host database.

McAdams, T., Freeman, J. and Pincus, L. (1995). Law, Business and Society (4th ed.). IL: Irwin.

Messer, S. (2007). Maximizing return from the 80-20 rule, American Marketing Association, Retrieved November 11, 2007 from http://www.marketing power.com/content16577.php.

Morgan, T. (1994). *Untying the knot of war: A bargaining theory of international crises.* Ann Arbor, MI: University of Michigan Press.

Morris, J., Brotherridge, C. and Urbanski, J. (2005), Bringing humility to leadership: Antecedents and consequences of leader humility, Human Relations, 58(10), 1323-1350. Retrieved April 24, 2007 from ProQuest database.

Newman, H.A. and Mozes, H.A. (1999), Does the Composition of Compensation Committee Influence CEO Compensation Practices, *Financial Management,* 28, 41-54.

Ohno, T. (1988). *Toyota production system: Beyond large-scale production,* Productivity Press: New York.

Parkinson, C. (1957). *Parkinson's law,* University of Malaya. Retrieve May 24, 2007 from http://lib.novgorod.net/DPEOPLE/PARKINSON/parkinson.txt

Piccoli, G. (2005). Review: IT-dependent strategic initiatives and sustained competitive advantage: A review and synthesis of the literature, *MIS Quarterly,* 29(4), 747-776. Retrieved April 24, 2007 from EBSCO database.

Rindova, V., Pollock, T., and Hayward, M. (2006). Celebrity firm's: The social construction of market popularity, *Academy of Management Review,* 31(1), 50-71. Retrieved April 24, 2006 from EBSCO host database.

Schwarber, P. (2005). Leaders and the decision-making process, *Management Decision,* 43(7/8), 1086-1092. Retreived on April 24, 2007 from Emerald database.

Scott, W. R. (2003). *Organizations: Rational, natural, and open systems* (5th ed.). Upper Saddle River, NJ: Prentice Hall.

Senge, P. (2006). *The fifth discipline: The art & Practice of the learning organization.* New York: Random House.

Shivdasani, A. and Yermack, D. (1999), CEO Involvement in the Selection of New Members: An Empirical Analysis, *Journal of Finance,* 54, 1829-1853.

Shriberg, A., Shriberg, D. L., and Lloyd, C. (2002). *Practicing leadership, principles and applications*. New York: John Wiley & Sons.

Thomas, H. (2003). An integration of thoughts and knowledge management, *Decision Sciences*, 34(2), 189-196. Retrieved April 24, 2007 from EBSCO Host database.

The Economist. Leaders: Another scandalous year. Business behavior. *The Economist*, 2003b, 369(8355), 14.

Time to boot celebrities, enact board reforms. (2005, November 28). Crain's Chicago Business, 28(48), 22. Retrieved April 29, 2007 from EBSCO database.

Turnbull, S. (1997). Stakeholder governance, *Corporate Governance*, (5), 11-23. Retrieved May 8, 2007 from ProQuest database.

Vafeas, N. (2003), Length of Board Tenure and Outside Director Independence, *Journal of Business Finance and Accounting* 30, 1043-1064.

Velasquez, M. (1998). *Business Ethics Concepts and Cases* (4th ed.). Upper Saddle River, NJ: Prentice-Hall.

Weisman, R. (2006, October 6). HP case likely to spur corporate change, *Boston Globe*, p. E.1. Retrieved April 24, 2007 from ProQuest database.

Williamson, O., Bercovitz, J., (1997). *The modern corporation as an efficiency instrument: The comparative contracting perspective*. In C. Kaysen (ed.), The American Corporation Today. New York: Oxford University Press.

Yermack, D. (1996), Higher Market Valuation of Companies with a Small Board of Directors, *Journal of Financial Economic*, 40, 185-211.

About the Authors

 Eric Yocam has accumulated over 15 years experience in industry. His pursuit is maintaining lifelong balance between scholar, practitioner and leader. As a researcher, his research interests are in the areas of information systems, corporate security, corporate governance, leadership, real option theory, and fuzzy logic.

He holds a master of science degree in computer science from the College of Engineering, Computer Science and Technology at California State University-Chico in Chico CA, a master of science degree in finance from the Albers School of Business and Economics at Seattle University in Seattle WA, a master of business administration degree from the School of Business Administration at the University of San Diego in San Diego CA, and a bachelor of science degree in computer engineering from the School of Engineering at the University of the Pacific in Stockton CA.

He also holds a "Certificate of Director Education", a nationally recognized designation for corporate directors confirmed in 2007 by the National Association for Corporate Directors (NACD) Corporate Directors Institute.

 Siu Kuen Annie Choi is a licensed attorney in the state of Washington. As a legal researcher, her research interests are in the areas of corporate governance, international business, and immigration law.

She holds a juris doctorate degree from Thomas Jefferson School of Law in San Diego CA, a master of international business degree from the School of Business Administration at the University of San Diego in San Diego CA, and a bachelor of business administration from the School of Business Administration at the University of San Diego in San Diego CA.

Send Us Feedback

Any and all feedback is welcome. The authors want to ensure that this publication stays current and at the forefront of capturing an authoritative source on corporate governance. To this end the authors encourage the reader's feedback on any topic found within this publication.

The authors would like the readers input for inclusion of additional key topics, and other important information that should be part of this publication.

Email feedback about this publication to *feedback@yocampublishing.com*

Yocam Publishing LLC

Information about upcoming publications by the authors of this work can be found at *http://www.yocampublishing.com*

Yocam Publishing LLC is a company committed to promoting awareness on various contemporary topics of interest, enriching professional best practice, and encouraging practical application from new findings relevant theoretical research.

NOTES

Index

theories of, 5–6
trends, 67–70
types of, 7*f*, 8–9, 83
governance index (G-index), 44–45, 82
Governance Institute, 63
Governance Metrics International
    (GMI), 9, 44, 46, 83
governance score (G-score), 45, 82
government regulations, 34
G-score (governance score), 45, 82

Harvard Business School Corporate
    Governance Initiative, 23
Health Insurance Portability and
    Accountability Act of 1996 (HIPPA),
    41–42, 83
health insurance regulations, 41–42
human resources committee, 28

iDashboards, 61
independent director, 16, 83
information needs of directors, 15
information technology, 70
insider trading, 21
Institute of Directors, 63
institutes for boards, 62–63
Institutional Shareholder Services (ISS),
    10, 44, 45
insurance for boards, 22
interconnected boards, 12–13, 83
interlocked boards, 12–13, 83
internal rate of return, 57
investment committee, 27
investment value, 83
Investor Responsibility Research Center
    (IRRC), 44, 45
ISS (International Shareholder Services),
    10, 44, 45

key performance indicators, 60, 84
KISS technique, 37

law suits, shareholder, 42

leadership roles
    defined, 84
    and directors, 18, 20
    impact of globalization, 67–68
    multicultural, 69
learning organizations, 55
liability insurance, 22

morality, 21, 84
multicultural leadership, 69

National Association of Corporate
    Directors (NACD), 24
net present value, 57
networking, 62–63
nominating committee, 9, 27
nonconformance, cost of, 53
non-executive director, 16, 84
non-profit organization, 8, 84

one-time costs, 57
organization models, 31–33
outside director, 84
overcommittment of directors, 24

Pareto Principle, 55
Patriot Act of 2001, 42
payouts, directors, 44
payouts, shareholders, 44
pensions and benefits committee, 27
performance measurements, 36–37
planning committee, 28
poison pill, 84
privately-held corporation, 8, 85
project constraints, 50–51
project duration, 58
public corporation, 8, 84
public policy committee, 27

quality, costs of, 53
quality improvement programs, 50–53

record keeping requirements, 42

978-0-595-45192-0
0-595-45192-6

Printed in the United States
103283LV00005B/496-516/P